# of a Lifetime

Poems of Love, Loss and Living

By David Crowley

Copyright David Crowley 2020

Published by Mejoma Publishing Co.
141 Pewabic Street
Laurium, MI 49913-2035

Cover Art by
Allyssa Cocciolone

Facebook David Crowley

Facebook David's Town Books

davidcrowley36@gmail.com

Introduction

In 1963 I was in the 6th grade at Sacred Heart Catholic School. My teacher, Mrs. Erskine, held a poetry contest in May, which is the month that the Catholic Church dedicates to the Blessed Virgin Mary. We were challenged to write a poem with the Blessed Virgin as the subject. My poem was chosen as the winner. Following that I was encouraged by Mrs. Erskine and my mother to continue writing. Over the next few years I wrote many poems, the majority of them silly musings of a pre-teen kid.

In high school I began to write more serious poems. Both the Vietnam War and the Cold War were in progress and I chose subjects that touched on war, the nuclear threat, the direction the world seemed to be taking and the generation gap. A number of my poems had themes of death or told ghostly stories to the extent that my then-girlfriend began to call me Edgar Allan Poe Jr.

I wrote very little for a number of years after high school. When I began again it was sporadic, the inspiration coming and going depending on what was happening in my life. The poems in this collection cover a period of more than fifty years. They are a small sample of what I've written during the course of my life since that first 6th grade attempt.

I am including my contest winning poem simply because it's the start of all the others in this book, not because I think it's a literary masterpiece. Please be gentle in your appraisal of an eleven year old's writing. I am also including two poems from my high school days as examples of my writing during that time. Following those first three poems the others appear in chronological order from the late 1970s to the present.

Some of the poems record local or national events. Others reflect my personal experiences and emotions. Quite a few tell of love in its many stages from finding to sharing to questioning to losing. A few are simply whimsical, aimed at hoping to make the reader smile. Most are self-explanatory but I have included an explanation for some of the event that inspired them.

My hope is that readers will find something in this collection that will touch them in some way. A poem will hopefully stir an emotion, cause a reader to see its subject from a new perspective, bring to mind a memory, or simply find enjoyment in the reading. Hopefully this book will provide a little of all those things.

Blessed Mother

Oh, Blessed Virgin, Queen of May,
guide me now right through the day.
On the first we crown thee Queen
so in need of help, on you we may lean.
I am not good, and not a saint.
A picture of you I cannot paint.
But in my mind I'll keep your face
and try to keep a holy pace.
Holy Mary, full of grace,
help me keep that holy pace.
And if I ever lose the trail
put me back on the holy rail.
The road to Heaven I cannot get on
unless I am innocent like a fawn.
When in trouble I'll call on you
to tell me then what I should do.
When I draw a very short breath,
when I know I'm close to death,
Mary let me pray to you
that I may walk on Heaven's dew.
When I'm gone, and gone for good,
people won't have a sorry mood.
Poems are made by fools like me,
but no one else is lovely as thee.

David Crowley
6th grade

— High School —

Stone Cold

Walls of stone, doors of steel,
tell the secret you conceal.
Open wide your bolted gate.
Whisper tales of love and hate.
Fling your shutters open wide.
Loose the prisoner you hide.
Speak, I cannot feel.
The key had been forgotten there.
I started slowly up the stair.
The night was shattered by the creak
of rusted hinges fain to speak.
I turned to leave, when from within
a voice cried out, "Forget your sin."
So ended there my final quest
to see where I'd been laid to rest.

Pray For The Repose
Of The Soul Of The World

The shadow of yesterday was swallowed by the night
as people hid their fears until tomorrow.
But in the morning in the soft grey light
they looked out, finding only sorrow.
Dressed in black they mourn the dead, the lost,
as reflections of their own lives pass before their eyes.
How much more is this life going to cost?
How many stories must be told; how many lies?
How many men must give their lives for justice,
when no one really cares or gives a damn?
How much more good must poor men miss
before we say "We are" and not "I am"?
How many lives must be lost before
we say "Enough. We want no more."?

I wrote this poem after a day in October in the late 1970s when I delivered mail in the neighborhood where I grew up

Autumn, Looking Back

Half-naked trees stand against
a grey sky backdrop.
Smells
of dead leaves
and apples
and wood smoke.
My love, my hideaway,
my autumn.
Your chill,
breathing on my face is my comfort.
Your witch-crossed moon
gives light to paths
where childhood memories run
in shadow.
And I,
sweater-wrapped against the wind,
walk,
where once I ran.

BE

Be as you are and change,
not as much for better
as for yourself.
Be as you perceive yourself,
not as much for pride
as for dignity.
Be as like to no one
as much as like to God,
not to know perfection
but to seek it.
Be not in fear of dying
lest life become a treasure
too valuable to spend.
Be not in fear of sorrow
lest you never know the strength
nor the wisdom born of tears.
Be as you were meant to be,
never losing sight of hope,
never taking more than you would give.
Be, not as much for being,
as for using well the time you have
to be.

Winter, Tread Softly

Winter, tread softly
past Autumn's golden grave.
She gave her life for you,
laying down her treasures
as your cold remorseless sword
cut through her heart.
Give honor to her resting place
for soon you will be lying by her side.

Spring, dance gaily
in your clean green garment
while your tears of joy fall freely
on the withered Winter's tomb.
Dance gaily with a bright bouquet
of newly opened flowers.
Dance freely, but do not forget
the lesson Winter taught before he died.

Summer, come warmly
with a sweet tempting smile.
Beguile the Spring with promises
of ripened fruit and brighter days.
Call her to your chamber
with your warm and gentle breezes.
Rob her of her innocence
before you take the life you cannot save.

Autumn, remember,
as you gild the green of Summer
and take upon yourself a crown
that once was his to wear,
that soon your strength will falter
and your crown will fall around you.
Stripped of all your glory
your fortune will be scattered,
and Winter will tread softly past your grave.

Your Children

We are the last, the final hour,
the one fresh breath of air.
We are your children.

Your dreams are ours, our dreams are yours,
you made us as we are.
We are your children.

Please don't let go, hold tight our hands,
lest we should slip away.
We are your children.

Our only chance is what you leave,
our hope is in your hands...

We were your children.

Farewell

Some evening in your solitude setting,
in seasons yet to pass,
remember what has gone before
our last good-byes are said.
Hold the memory gently,
as a butterfly cupped in your hand,
and think of me,
for I will think of you.

Clouds After Rain

Sunlight on clouds after rain.
In the train of days this one
has passed. Wet and awful
for this time of year. At last
the sun may have its moment.

Moonlight on small inland lakes.
It will take until tomorrow
to dry the puddled streets.
They've yet another night to cry
out on the tear-streaked pavement.

Read This Book Backwards

Read this book backwards.
I know that sounds strange,
but the ending is really quite good.
And I know the beginning's
a tiny bit weak.
I wrote it the best that I could.
The last page is really
where I should have started.
The first page is really the end.
I'm not really sure now
where I got mixed up.
It wasn't what I had intend-
ed . . . Oh, damn!

For children living in an unhappy home
whose parents don't see the damage they do.

Whispered Hallways

I heard the whispered hallways and the music,
not unlike the leaves in Autumn's midst,
soft to the earth in gentle mystery
when the moon hides their secret travels
and their footsteps sing a distant song.
Tears, more tears, for the shattered silence
where sleep once found uneasy comfort.
Tears, more tears, for the lonely child
to whom the whispered hallways show no mercy.
Tears, more tears, for the whispered hallways,
who cannot in the darkness see the tears.

I Will

I will see beyond the mountains.
I will hear above the thunder.
I will ever keep a vigil by your side.
I will touch you with my memories.
I will hold you with my dreams.
I will wait for you when all the world has died.

I May Yet In The Winter

I may yet in the winter be warm
and unnoticed by the white whispering
when the chill has crushed the bones of friends
and left them for dead.
I may yet walk the perilous path
long forsaken to the crystal treachery,
feared by the flesh whose spirit
chose to stay in bed.

I may yet in the winter be warm
by the fire from the still-green wood
when the dry wood has been spent
and its ashes cold.
I may yet in the long night find comfort
in the bosom of the soft young bed
while the white whisper warns the window
of the death foretold.

I may yet in the winter be warm
and forgotten as the frost fantasy
covers the warm brown earth and the stain
where my spirit bled.
I may yet, when the dark invades the day
and the brave light briefly stands its ground,
close my eyes beneath the pale blanket
and sleep in peace instead.

Together/Apart

Worlds

apart.

Living together.

Sharing the same space.

Having nothing

in common.

Strangers

who know each other

better than anyone.

Were we?

Are we?

When will it

end?

Closing Night

Now the end must fall
as the curtain at the last curtain call.
Never to rise again,
hiding the eyes of the cast.
This run has passed too quickly.
Dismantle the lights!
Strike this set, this canvas
upon which we painted our world,
forgetting that the surface
was that and nothing more.

Now the theater is empty.
Only the echo of footsteps is heard
as I cross down center for one whispered word
of good-bye as the stage door closes.

This was written after seeing a TV report about an explosion at a school in the Basque country.

The Basque School Explosion
10/23/80

First I heard the noise,
so loud it hurt my ears.
Everyone was screaming
and running. Split-second fears,
then the silence.

Why are the walls so heavy?
Am I the only one?
No, I hear their voices,
my friends are calling me to run
and play among the ruins.

Our parents are digging.
Their tears fall warm
upon the shattered stone.
Out in the midday sun
they all seem so alone,
while we lie here together
with the friends that we have known.

Mama, God *is* beautiful!
MAMA!!!

The House Around Me

The house around me has a way
of holding on to memories.
It has a life within its walls
we humans do not know.
Beneath the painted surface
the wooden bones and plaster flesh
protect its quiet secret.
To leave this house
would be to leave a friend.
So often have we sat together
telling tales. Spinning songs
on wheels of hope and promise,
one slender silver thread
to hang our lives on.
This house and I are brothers,
life's greatest moments shared.
The sorrow and the joy of years
lie hidden in these walls.
Our lives will one day separate
as lives are prone to do.
Yet here will live a part of me
till wood and stone
are ash and sand
and memories have died.

Side By Side

Now it's good to have some faith in one's own ability,
but it takes quite a feat of athletic agility
to stand side by side with oneself.

Communication Gap

I can hear you
but I don't know what you're saying.

What's wrong with you?

The Magician

He conjures up the visions
while their eyes expand to see.
Though it's only an illusion,
it's a child's reality.

Sweet Surrender

There on the square of muslin and cotton,
bordered by loneliness, sheltered from light,
we meet in the shadows of uncertain trust
and the darkness of uncertain passion.
The lies that protect us are tactfully lost
in the whispers of promises never fulfilled.
The truth that betrays us is hidden behind
the smiling self-portrait we fashion.
In half-naked stanzas of unfinished songs
we touch for a moment. My hand on your skin
feels the warmth of the woman, the joy of the child;
my lips taste your swift sweet surrender.
We struggle to savor what little is left
of the gilded illusions that once filled our eyes.
As we gather up fragments of clothing and dreams
we whisper good-byes neither cruel nor tender.

Coward Eyes

As if love were not enough there must be pain
and once again the battered broken promise,
forgotten, or forgiven of its deeds.
In a passing silent moment your eyes cower
from the presence of the misbegotten trust.

Damn these eyes who cannot look away!

I dare not be and yet I am
and being so the trust has been deceived,
plundered not of truth but of itself.
Oh, wasted love, you bear the shame of sin
because you cannot cry in public places.

Each time I see your eyes again
my tears are not enough to wash
my simple sin away.
Between us stands the broken trust,
the promise unfulfilled,
not by our fault, but by our chosen fate.

Your coward eyes are really not,
they merely fear themselves.
So you must turn away again
before you see the pain,
and in the silence love must be enough.

Seasons of a Lifetime

These next two poems won grand prizes in national poetry contests. The first is self-explanatory.

The second was written when Jessica McClure was stuck in a well in Texas for several days. My youngest daughter was about the same age so I felt a strong parental empathy with what was happening. A poem about the second shuttle disaster can be found on a later page.

Challenger 1/28/86

It would soar to the edge of infinity,
this thunderous white dove,
through the ice-blue morning air of expectation.
Toward a realm of freedom it rose once more;
a trail of white, a flash of fire, a sudden chilling stillness.
And the seven fell from the face of God
into his outstretched arms.

Where are you now, you ambassadors of dreams?
Have you seen the stars? Have you touched them?
You have traveled through spaces unknown to us here,
far beyond what you thought were your limits and goals,
to a place and a time called forever.
You would teach us, and yes, we have learned from you now,
though the lessons are painful and sad.
You have taught us of courage. You have taught us of strength.
You have taught us to reach for the stars, to have faith.

Sail on, you seven, you brave chosen few.
You belong now to the heavens, they belong now to you.

Jessica In The Darkness

Jessica in the darkness, no place to lay your head;
no mother's arms to hold you, no softness in your bed.
You hear your mother calling but you cannot see her face.
You can't reach out to touch her in this dark forbidding place.
And so you dream of Pooh Bear and sing to ease the pain.
Then those above who love you know their efforts aren't in vain.
The hours pass so slowly and the stone seems so unfair.
Your fingers find a refuge in your soft familiar hair.
From all around the angels have now gathered at your side
to guard you in the darkness and to dry the tears you've cried.
Sleep now, tiny damsel. Rest your weary mind.
The angels bring the promise that God is not unkind.

The sound is getting closer and you wonder what it is.
Then someone's hand is touching you and you are touching his.
But now there must be pain again to slowly get you out.
You feel him gently pulling but your mind is filled with doubt.

The dark gives way to brilliant light, you hear the people cheer.
Soon you feel the comfort of your parents standing near.
The gathered angels smile as they return to where they'd been,
for the littlest of angels is among us once again.
Jessica in the darkness, you never were alone.
The angels and a million prayers were with you on that stone.

October 20, 1987

Seasons

Where will you go in the season
when the last leaf has left the limb
and fallen to its golden death?

When the white-frocked orphans dance in mid-air
while their siblings lie spent on the frozen ground
how will I follow your footsteps?

After the new buds break from their bondage
and the green returns to the forest
will you walk through my garden unnoticed
while the moon seeps in through the curtains
and spills on the floor with my dreams?

When the fruit hangs ripe on the burdened bough
and the wheat waves tall in the field
will I turn toward the sun
and, blinded, miss you
running beyond a distant hill?

When my bed lies wasted beside me,
and the days and the years become one,
I will lie down to die with your name on my lips.
As the seasons pass, so must the man.

The Story Lost It's Meaning

You sit,
or more correctly, recline,
on the couch in the corner;
captured by the window,
or perhaps by the bird on the branch outside.
Lost for the moment,
lost for all time,
for time has no measure on this day.

We stopped in mid-sentence
when the bird caught your eye.
The words hung half-finished in the stillness
while the story lost its meaning.

Now we've lost our place.
I wonder if it's time to put the book away.

Look For Just A Moment

Look for just a moment. Run and hide your eyes.
Words of consolation aren't enough for our good-byes.
I'm searching for a reason for dreams that don't come true.
Every time I close my eyes your face comes into view.
Without a happy ending the story ends the same;
a once forgotten lover, a once remembered name.
A time too short for waiting, a time that must be shared;
a dream that held a meaning for which you weren't prepared.
Look for just a moment. Turn before you see
the remnants of the man I thought that I would be.

3:00 AM

Time never passes
as slowly
as it does
on the nights
when we can't
sleep.

Night Song

We awoke to the sound of our hearts
pounding in the darkness.
I turned away when I felt your hand
fall like a feather on my shoulder.
I felt old then,
as if the night would pass too quickly.
If I turned to hold you
would you see the years in my face
even in the darkness?
Would you feel the fear in my hands,
or the faltering pride in my arms?
I could cry like a child
but the child has died.
He lies, now,
buried in the darkness.

You beg to see the truth in me
while my heart is slow to turn.
My truth is far too arrogant,
too empty in its self-deceit,
too wrapped in remorse to break its silence.
Lost within my shadowed soul
it broods. More from its fear it lies
hidden, as a child would hide,
somewhere in the darkness.

A music video showed a bed where people kept appearing on and off in various poses; playing guitar, reading, sleeping, crying, etc. I found myself thinking they were like ghosts in a bed.

Ghost In My Bed

The rustling of sheets
breaks my cold restless sleep,
drawing me to your arms.
I reach through the darkness
where emptiness lingers
and slowly a memory stirs.
I feel you beside me
where only the air
lies waiting to taunt
my outstretched arms.
I hear you close by me
where only the sound
of my breath
can be heard in the room.
Sheets rise and fall
where your spirit remains;
your pillow still cradles your head.
There are you always
when night closes in,
where your arms wait to hold me
and love me again.

Give The Night To Morning

Give the night to morning,
let your sadness slip away.

When dawn bathes the blackened walls,
washing the shadows from your wounded heart,
turn your eyes to the far horizon
and your back to the unkind memory.

Sing the Summer Solstice
when the aging night weakens
and barely stands before it falls
under the morning's sword.
Raise your head from your tear-washed hands
to the scarlet sky of hope.

Accept from the day its promise
of strength to withstand the darkness.
Offer in return your troubled dreams
whose heavy hands torment your sleep
with their callous crude caress.

Set your course for morning,
let the darkness fall behind you.
Let the night slip through your fingers
as the morning takes your hand.

I wrote this in 1993 after seeing a news report during the Yugoslavian war. It showed a bombed out area where in a window in one of the few buildings left standing a young boy could be seen staring out at the wasteland around him.

Face In A Window

His eyes behind the jagged glass
show no sign of life.
They stare at empty streets
and stumps
where leaves will never grow again.
Perhaps there was a tear there once,
but that was long ago.
Now the tears are dry and best forgotten.

His lips are firmly set,
determined not to quiver;
showing strength, with just a hint
of weary resignation.
They never move, yet tell a tale
that mourns the country's shame.

Below the ragged uncombed hair
his ears stick out a little.
The sound of distant gunfire
goes unnoticed after all this time.
The laughter of his friends at school
is now a silent memory.
There's hunger in his sunken cheeks,
confusion on his brow.
Tomorrow, if it comes, will be the same.

He turns away, and as he does
his shoulders show the burden
that weighs upon the child
and drives his childhood from his heart.

As he leaves a curtain falls,
continuing the story
empty windows, empty lives,
the price of empty glory.

Holding You

I held you for a moment,
not long enough, but longer
than my heart should dare to ask
or be permitted.
My arms held tightly, stubbornly
resisting all my efforts
to force them to abandon
the treasure they had found.
They memorized each feeling;
each gentle curve, each breath,
to savor in the days to come
when I have need of comfort.
My trembling hands found strength in you,
my soul was filled with wonder
to know your heart was beating next to mine.

If somewhere in that moment
as we touched our minds were one,
then you would know that what I say is true.
You'd know the depth of all I feel;
you'd see my dreams, my fears.
You'd understand my longing
to be always holding you.

Last Touch

Turn from me
when the passing moment
slips beyond our reach.
Promise to return again
for I am naught without you.

The feel of your last touch
lingered gently on my skin,
a bittersweet reminder
of your presence.
Your sweet uncertain smile
danced within my wishful heart
as you were fading softly
in the distance.

Hold in your heart the joy of the moment.
Hold in your soul the spirit.

Awakening

You told me that the morning
was not a time to look on you,
and yet my greatest dream remains
to see you when you wake;
to watch the sunlight softly fall
across your sleeping face
and know you were beside me
in the darkness as I slept.

I long to see your tousled hair
adorn the pillow next to mine;
to hear your quiet breathing
like a distant summer breeze.
I long to feel your body stir
beside me in the shadows,
remembering the evening
and the promise that was kept.

I'd reach to touch your silken skin,
enfold your morning warmth in mine.
I'd kiss your gentle smile
and your sleepy half-awakened eyes.
I'd marvel at your softness,
tears of joy would fill my eyes.
Throughout the day I'd cherish then
the memory of the tears I wept.

Morning

I'd bring your morning coffee
as you rested on the bed
where our legs had intertwined so easily.
When last I lay beside you
I kissed the slumber from your eyes,
caressed your supple shoulders
and the arms that held my dreams.
We'd sit and talk of yesterday
and what today might bring us.
I'd thank you for the evening
and the promise we had shared.
My eyes would fill with ecstacy
to see your beauty waiting there,
your naked body dark
against the sunlight on the sheets.
One kiss, one touch, to ease the pain
of leaving as I said good-bye
to face an endless day without you near.
I'd whisper that I love you
as I held my inspiration
tightly in my arms
to give me strength to face the day.
The morning would remain with me,
your face before me always,
until the evening in its mercy
brought me home to you.

Evening

A quiet falls upon the world;
the sounds of life grow distant
as shades are drawn and shadows
stretch across the kitchen floor.
Your heartbeat would surround me then,
filling me with gratitude
that I have been so blessed
to even once have held you in my arms.
Together we would sip our wine,
made sweeter by the taste of you
that lingered on my lips
and left me thirsting yet for more.
Your hands would gently touch my chest;
your smile would touch my being
as you wiped away the day's remains
with the sweetness of your charms.
I'd settle on the couch
and draw your body close beside me,
holding once again the dream
that gives my life its reason.
As darkness fell around us there
we'd share again the promise
that brings true meaning to our love
through every passing season.

Nightfall

The bedroom walls surround us
with a moonlight painted fresco;
an ever-changing still life
of dancing leafy limbs.
Your softness in the darkness
brings comfort as I hold you,
thanking God again
that I was blessed to know your love.
Our bodies move in harmony,
a song that only we will hear;
a melody of silent touch
and breathless feathered kisses.
Your warmth engulfs my senses
as the promise leads my soul
to be the love you long for,
whose promise lasts forever.
My hand becomes your truest friend,
never letting go of you;
firmly guiding all your hopes,
gently guarding all your dreams.
The promise lives within us there,
our bodies now as one;
our heartbeats joined in rhythm;
one breath, one life, one soul.
As sleep descends to cover us
with peaceful satisfaction
I look with joy toward morning
to be there for your awakening.

The Promise Kept

Your skin was cool
as you pressed your back
against my chest for comfort,
not knowing that the comfort was my own.
I felt the joy
of the promise kept;
the pleasure of your softness,
a greater peace than any I had known.

Your sighs were soft
as I held you close
while my hands caressed your beauty.
You whispered "Please don't leave me." as we lay.
I doubt you knew
as you spoke those words
they would live with me forever
to keep you near when I must stay away.

If

If all the world were mine
but I could never see your face,
I'd give it all away for just
one day in your embrace.

If God stood here before me
and offered me his power,
I'd ask instead to hold you
in my arms for just an hour.

If I could ask for anything
except to be with you,
I'd stand in hopeless silence
till my lonely life was through.

Let My Love Enfold You

Let my love enfold you,
let my faithfulness become the rock
where you may safely rest above the rising tide.

Let my love enfold you,
let my steadfastness become your shield,
guarding you from all the ghosts
of countless broken promises.

Let my love enfold you
with a promise that will never fail;
a gentle hand to break your fall,
a heart that sees no other,
a man, no more or less,
and yet a man whose love is true.

Prayer For My Best Friend

May there always be love on the path that you travel.
May there always be hope in the wind in the trees.
May you ever find Spring at the end of your Winter.
May a safe harbor greet you in turbulent seas.

May your memories be kind when they sit down beside you.
May your heart never falter when Truth comes to call.
May your dreams guide your steps when the way is uncertain.
May my words lift you up when you stumble and fall.

May you know in your soul that I never will leave you.
May you hear in the silence my breath in the air.
May you never know fear. May your constant companion
be my prayer that entrusts you to God's tender care.

Almost Home
(for the Shuttle Columbia, 2/2003)

Homeward, ever homeward,
almost home and flying
high above the home you love.
Spirits soaring,
hearts on fire,
soon you'll hear the voices
and see the smiles of those who wait;
it seems you've been so long away.

But something isn't right now.
No, something's very wrong.
It breaks into your reverie,
then breaks your hearts and dreams,
while here below our hearts are shattered
watching as the broken pieces
scatter all your broken dreams
across the saddened earth;
scars upon the memory of this day.

One last flight to glory,
a bright star in the clear blue sky
that writes your final story
in a trail of white as you pass by;
no longer almost home,
you're home with God.

Darkness

In the darkness I still feel you,
a soft caress along my arm,
a warm breeze on my shoulder
where your breath once fell
in gentle sighs of comfort
and regret.
I held you only long enough
to break your heart
and mine;
to fill me with your beauty,
then leave me lying helpless
in the darkness,
where I feel you,
where I love you,
where I die.

Away From You

I cannot turn away from you
without a sense of loss.
My eyes are filled with tears
when they no longer see your face.

Each moment I'm away from you
is filled with constant longing,
and worst of all,
a moment gone forever.

My heart is not away from you,
no matter where I am.
It stands beside you always
and will not leave your side.
It's there, where I want most of all to be.

Just A Boy (Aleppo 8/16)

His feet don't reach the floor;
they're barely able to hang over
the edge of the seat
where he's sitting alone
with a tear at the edge of his eye.
His face is covered
with dirt and blood,
and innocent confusion.
No trace of fear or sadness,
just a boy who wonders why.
And his questions
are our questions;
his confusion our alarm.
Just a boy, bewildered,
wondering,
asking us why no one came
to keep him safe from harm.

Girl From The Rubble (10/16)

Blood on her face;
blood on our conscience;
blood on the hands
of those who could save her.
Crying in fear;
crying for Daddy;
wearing the scars
of the war the world gave her.
Little girl lost,
pulled from the rubble;
once was a child,
now her childhood's gone.
Blood on her face.
How can you see her
without asking why
we still let this go on?

Dragons

I don't know why
the dragons fly
each night within my dreams.
For when I try
to ask them why
they answer me with screams
and screeches loud
that shake a cloud
and make its rain fall out.
So I believe
they'll only leave
when I learn how to shout.

Rude Awakening

To hear the wind
you'd think the world was ending.
How have the trees not cracked
from constant bending.
The timbers of the house cry out.
"We cannot stand much more!" they shout.
"God give us strength to bear this blow you're sending."

The sky's alive
with crisscrossed streaks of lightning.
The thunder's endless roar
is more than frightening.
The storm begins to fade at last.
It seems the worst of it has past,
and in the east the morning sky is brightening.

That Dream Of You

It came again,
that dream of you,
last night while I lay sleeping.
And in the dark
I heard my heart
break, and I woke weeping.
So many years
have passed since you
said we must part forever.
Yet in my dreams
we meet once more,
a love no years can sever.

I Wonder
(on a sleepless night)

I wonder
will you hear my voice
at night
while you lie sleeping?
Whispering "I love you".
Singing softly at your ear.

I wonder
when I'm gone
will you remember me
in sorrow?
Or will the love you found in me
seem no more than a dream?

I wonder
while you sleep
will you awake to find tomorrow
all memory of me
carried off
like leaves upon a stream?

I wonder
as I lie beneath the earth
will memories wake you,
your slumber broken
by your gentle weeping?
Or will the silence in your bed
be the answer that I fear?

Some poems written during the pandemic.

And So It Goes

Each day's the same, and so it goes,
and goes and goes and goes.
I watch TV. I watch the clock.
I count again my toes.
I dust the shelf I dusted
I think just yesterday.
It might have been the day before
or earlier today.
I wish I had a room to paint
so I could watch it dry.
Or maybe I could watch the sun
go slowly 'cross the sky
to see how far it travels
when an hour or so has passed.
I could, of course, reorganize
my cabinets at last.
But then again, I'm still alive
despite the ills and woes.
There's still a jigsaw puzzle
I can build. And so it goes.

April 3, 2020.

The Day Begins
(for the frontline heroes)

The day begins as always.
With luck, a cup of coffee waits.
Perhaps someone brought donuts,
but those are often gone too soon.
You don your suit of armor,
your cotton fabric breastplate,
your shield, your gloves'
your face mask,
the one you saved from yesterday.
Into the fray,
the crowded hallways,
searching for familiar faces,
saddened when they're gone
from where you saw them yesterday.
New faces have replaced them,
new lives for you to save,
or try, at least,
with all the strength you have.
This dragon breathes its fire
and scorches all it touches,
yet you withstand the flames
and fight as long as you can stand.
Ten hours later, maybe twelve,
or even more, who knows,
you lay your head down,
rest until
the day begins as always.

April 20, 2020

Home Alone 2020

They're home alone and frightened,
uncertain of the future.
Frustration simmers, anger builds,
while rumors running rampant
spread like flames across a forest,
fueling the uncertainty
and leaving naught but ashes
in their wake as they roar by.

For some there is sadness
beyond consolation
as loved ones must linger
to die all alone.
For others their hunger
hangs heavy upon them,
with fears of tomorrow
and what it will bring.
Some hold on with hands
gripping tightly to hope,
often just fingertips
hold them in place.
Some speak of their civil rights
taken unjustly.
They march in the streets
shouting slogans and hatred.
Simmered frustrations must come to a boil.

We pray in our homes
for a brighter tomorrow,
a time when we welcome
our families and friends
to gather our hopes
and our dreams for the future,
to cherish the freedom
we once took for granted,
looking forward to all
that tomorrow will bring.

April 21, 2020

Face In A Window 2020

She sits in a chair by the window
and watches the street outside,
hoping to see something happen,
a car driving by,
a man walking his dog.
She's not sure why she can't go out there,
or why no one comes over to play.
She only can look out the window
and hope that tomorrow
her grandma and grandpa
will stop by and visit
and blow her a kiss
while they stand on the steps of the porch.
Tomorrow, her mom says,
they'll play in the yard,
or maybe they'll go for a walk.
She knows there's a virus,
whatever that is,
she just knows that it's not very good.
And it's left her alone
with her mom and her dad
to just sit in a chair by the window
or play in the yard by herself,
hoping the virus will soon go away
and allow her to wake up one morning
and just be a child once again.

April 30, 2020

Quarantine Roommates

A new thing has happened,
I'm talking to things;
inanimate objects,
my keys and my key rings.
And pots on the stove
taking too long to bubble.
I scold them and tell them
they're really in trouble.
I talk to the TV,
it even replies,
but I'm not really sure
if it's telling me lies.
If I looked in the mirror
I could talk to myself.
But who wants to talk
to a grungy old elf?
The pictures I have
of my children might do.
Since they couldn't talk back
it would be something new.
So I sit here and wonder
what else can I find
to be my companion
so I don't lose my mind.

May 14, 2020

Seasons of a Lifetime

Teardrops Fell
(Earth Day 2020)

And all around me teardrops fell,
the tears of those whose sadness grew
as humankind destroyed the earth.
They fell in torrents, pouring down
on land too dry to welcome them
and flowed into a darkened sea
that not so long ago became
the grave of its inhabitants.
The tears touched hills where trees once stood
and trickled down the rocky slopes
that in the past were bright green meadows,
now forgotten, lost to memories
handed down by those who once
had seen the colors, smelled the fragrance
which so few still now recall.
And as the teardrops fell around me
I was taken back to when
the sky was blue, the air was clear,
and rain was merely drops of water
falling softly on the earth,
not tears that fell from eyes of angels
weeping for the world's demise.

One And Only

I've waited all these years,
and yet I'd wait another lifetime
for I will never find
another woman I could love.
So many times I've tried
only to find I was mistaken,
and all the words I wrote
were really meant for you alone.
And now the time has passed
and I must face the truth I've hidden
behind the fragile smile
that has protected me so long.
There is no hope for me
for I am left to love forever
the one and only love
my heart and soul have ever known.

One final thought.

Life, in a moment, is gone.

Love in a moment lives on.

Seasons of a Lifetime

David Crowley resides in Laurium, Michigan, a small town on the Keweenaw Peninsula (known as the Copper Country) in Michigan's Upper Peninsula. He retired from the United States Postal Service in December 2006. At the time of his retirement he was the Postmaster of Lake Linden, Michigan.

He has been writing poetry since 6th grade. Two of his poems have won Grand Prize awards in national poetry contests. In 2004 he published "Somewhere Waits An Angel," a collection of love poems.

He has published three rhyming children's books, "Twinkle Town," "This Town Ain't Big Enough" and "The Town That Lost Christmas." He has also written three full length plays and one one act play and is currently working on a full length murder mystery.

In addition to writing his interests include, singing, acting, directing plays and musicals, theatrical lighting design, cooking and baking. He was the play director for the Houghton Middle and High Schools from 2007 to 2020. In 2020 he took the position of play director for the Hancock Middle and High Schools to start a theater program there.

David has three children, Megan, Josh and Mallory, two grandsons, Noah and Samuel and a granddaughter, Alexis. He also has two step-grandsons, Aiden and Brantlee.

Children's books by David Crowley available on Amazon:

"This Town Ain't Big Enough" — A bully learns a lesson about friendship.

"The Town That Lost Christmas" — A young girl helps the people in her town remember the true meaning of Christmas.